STAR WARS™
WORKBOOKS

ABC FUN

FOR AGES 4–5

BY THE EDITORS OF BRAIN QUEST

■SCHOLASTIC

Scholastic Children's Books
Euston House,
24 Eversholt Street,
London NW1 1DB, UK

A division of Scholastic Ltd
London ~ New York ~ Toronto ~ Sydney ~ Auckland
Mexico City ~ New Delhi ~ Hong Kong

First published in the USA by Workman Publishing in 2014.
This edition published in the UK by Scholastic Ltd in 2015.

© & TM 2015 LUCASFILM LTD.

STAR WARS is a registered trademark of Lucasfilm Ltd.
BRAIN QUEST is a registered trademark of Workman Publishing Co., Inc., and Groupe Play Bac, S.A.

Workbook series design by Raquel Jaramillo
Cover illustration by Mike Sutfin
Interior illustrations by Joe Bartos, Eric Battle, Bret Blevins, Pat Pigott, Grant Gould and Ben Caldwell

ISBN 978 1407 16277 5

Printed and bound by Bell & Bain Ltd, United Kingdom

6 8 10 9 7 5

www.scholastic.co.uk

WORKBOOKS

This workbook belongs to:

_____

Can you sing the ABC song?

Point to all the letters in the boxes as you sing the ABC song.

Circle the boxes that spell your name!

A B C D
E F G H I
J K L M
N O P Q R
S T U V
W X Y Z

A

Anakin Skywalker

Anakin Skywalker begins with the capital letter **A**.

Colour the boxes that show a capital letter **A**.

A	B	A	F	A	D
A	E	D	A	A	C

acklay

The word **acklay** begins with the lowercase letter **a**.

a

Colour the circles that show a lowercase letter **a**.

(a) (a) (d) (a) (c) (a)

(c) (a) (b) (a) (e) (d)

B

Boba Fett

Boba Fett begins with the capital letter **B**.

Colour the boxes that show a capital letter **B**.

B	E	B	B	A	A
E	B	D	D	B	B

bantha

The word **bantha** begins with the lowercase letter **b**.

b

Colour the circles that show a lowercase letter **b**.

b   b   h   f   d   b

c   d   b   b   b   a

C

Count Dooku

Count Dooku begins with the capital letter **C**.

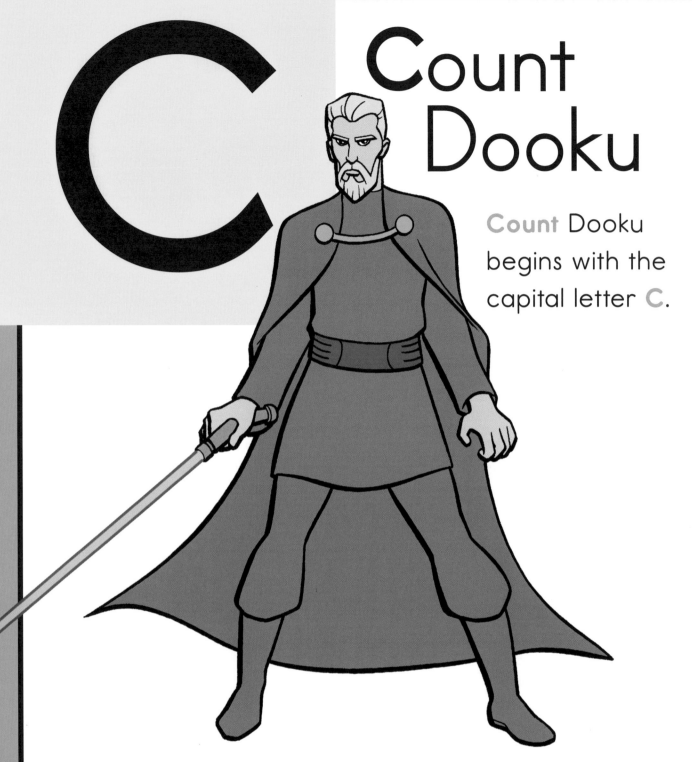

Colour the boxes that show a capital letter **C**.

C	A	G	E	C	C

G	C	C	C	D	B

clone trooper

C

The word **clone** begins with the lowercase letter **c**.

Colour the circles that show a lowercase letter **c**.

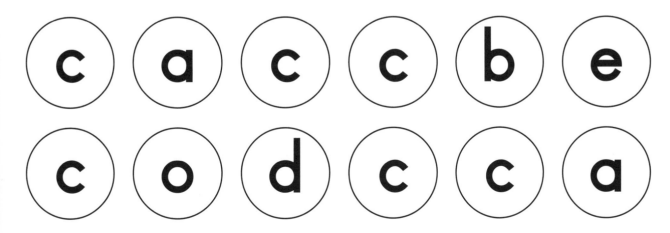

c a c c b e

c o d c c a

D

Darth Maul

Darth Maul begins with the capital letter **D**.

Colour the boxes that show a capital letter **D**.

D	C	B	A	H	D
E	D	D	D	D	F

droid

The word **droid** begins with the lowercase letter **d**.

Colour the circles that show a lowercase letter **d**.

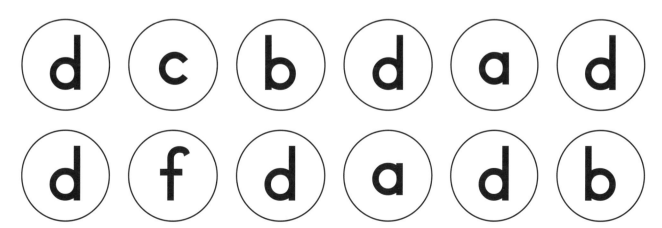

d c b d a d

d f d a d b

E

Emperor Palpatine

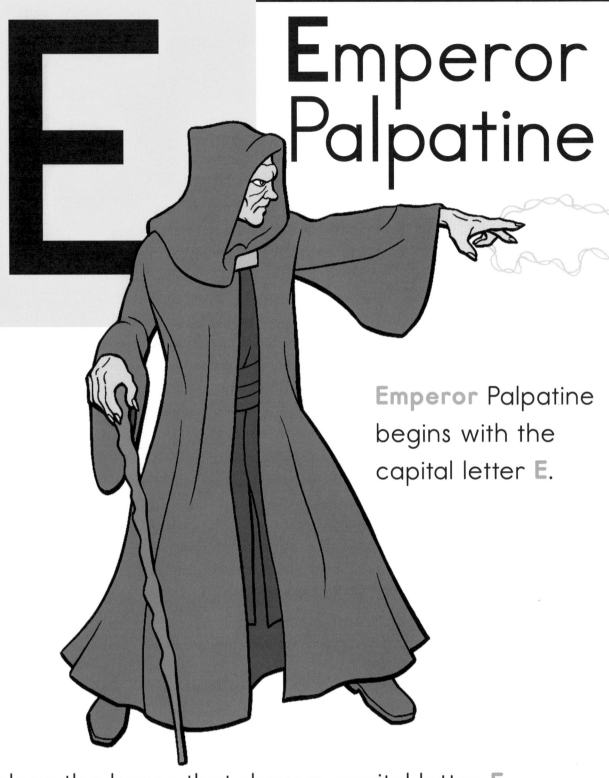

Emperor Palpatine begins with the capital letter E.

Colour the boxes that show a capital letter E.

E	B	E	A	E	F
E	D	F	E	H	E

escape pod

The word **escape** begins with the lowercase letter **e**.

Colour the circles that show a lowercase letter **e**.

e a c e b o

h e a e e e

F

Fisto

Kit **Fisto**'s last name begins with the capital letter **F**.

Colour the boxes that show a capital letter **F**.

F	B	A	F	H	B
F	E	F	E	F	F

fish

The word **fish** begins with
the lowercase letter **f**.

f

Colour the circles that show a lowercase letter **f**.

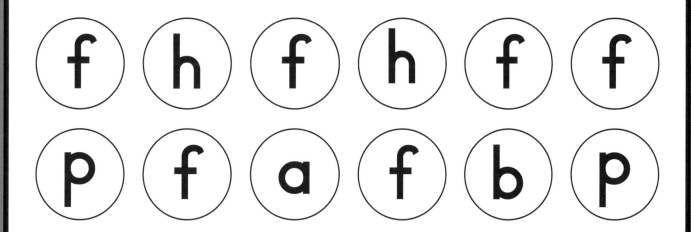

G Grievous

Grievous begins with the capital letter **G**.

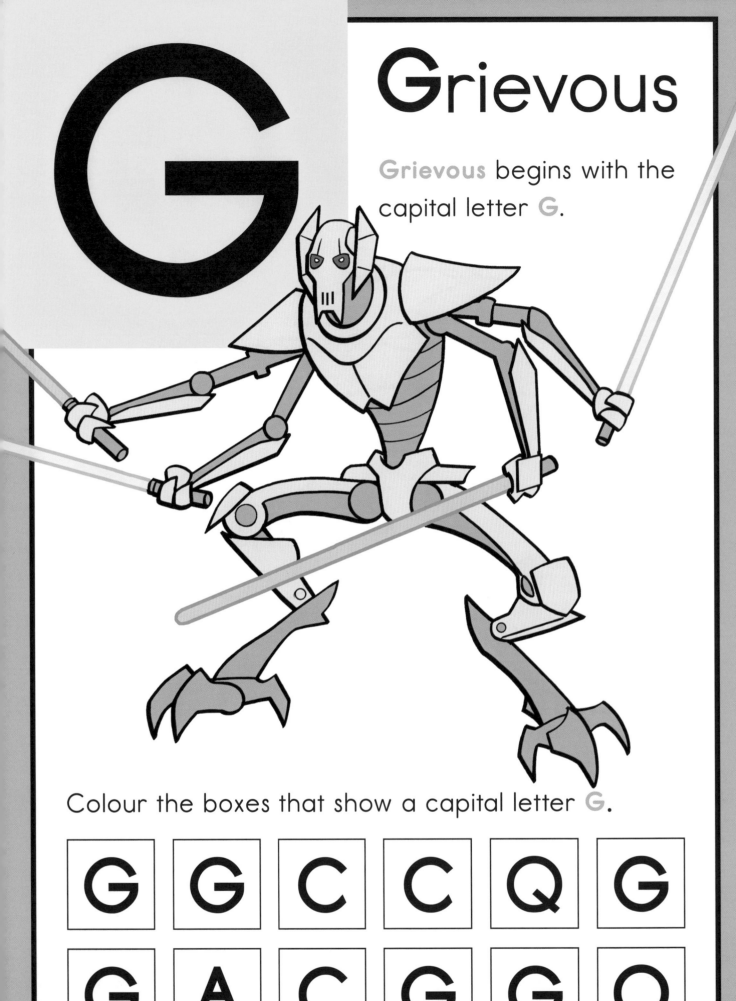

Colour the boxes that show a capital letter **G**.

G	G	C	C	Q	G
G	A	C	G	G	O

galaxy

The word **galaxy** begins with the lowercase letter **g**.

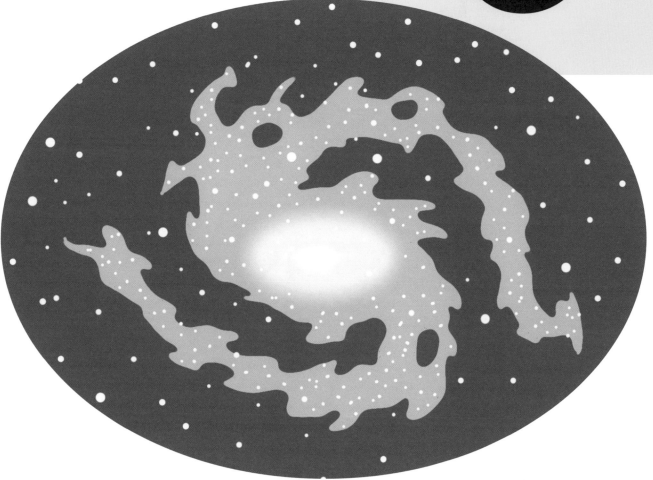

Colour the circles that show a lowercase letter **g**.

b a g a c g

g g b g g q

H

Han Solo

Han Solo begins with the capital letter H.

Colour the boxes that show a capital letter H.

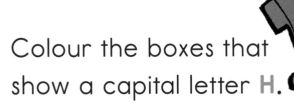

H	F	A	P	E	H
H	H	E	H	N	H

human

The word **human** begins with the lowercase letter **h**.

Colour the circles that show a lowercase letter **h**.

b h n h h f

h b h b a h

I

Imperial Guard

Imperial Guard begins with the capital letter **I**.

Colour the boxes that show a capital letter **I**.

I	I
E	T
I	I

L	F
J	I
I	F

insect

The word **insect** begins with the lowercase letter **i**.

Colour the circles that show a lowercase letter **i**.

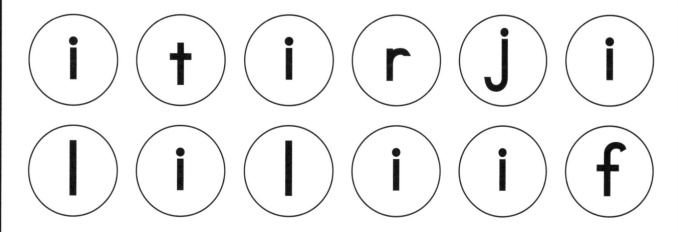

i   t   i   r   J   j

l   i   l   i   i   f

Let's play match-up!

On the opposite page, say the word for each picture.

What beginning sound do you hear?

Draw a line from each picture to its matching letter.

J

Jar Jar Binks

Jar Jar Binks begins with the capital letter J.

Colour the boxes that show a capital letter J.

J	J	J	P	U	J
U	J	L	B	J	C

jet pack

j

J

The word **jet** begins with the lowercase letter **j**.

Colour the circles that show a lowercase letter **j**.

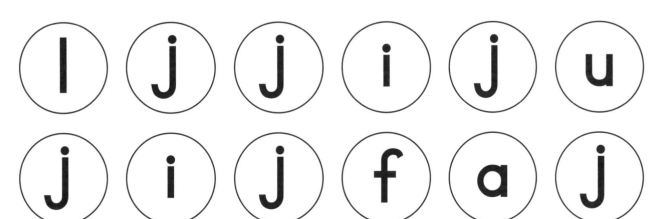

l J j i j u

j i j f a j

K

Ki-Adi-Mundi

Ki-Adi-Mundi
begins with
the capital letter **K**.

Colour the boxes that show a capital letter **K**.

H	P	K	Y	K	K
K	K	F	B	K	Z

kaadu

The word **kaadu** begins
with the lowercase letter **k**.

k

Colour the circles that show a lowercase letter **k**.

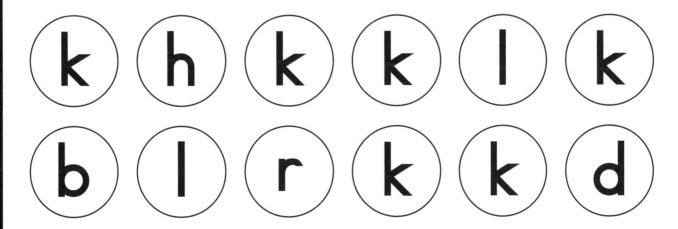

L

Luke Skywalker

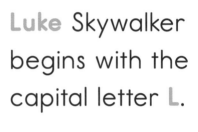

Luke Skywalker begins with the capital letter L.

Colour the boxes that show a capital letter L.

L	E	K	L	T	L
H	L	N	F	L	L

lizard

The word **lizard** begins
with the lowercase letter **l**.

Colour the circles that show a lowercase letter **l**.

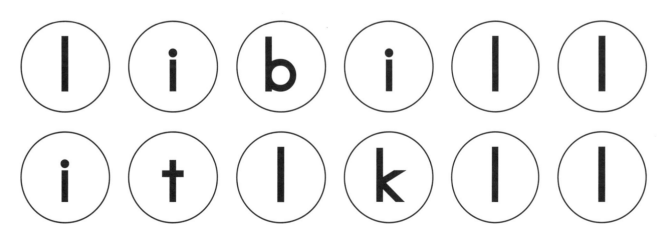

l i b i l l

i t l k l l

M

Mace Windu

Mace Windu begins with the capital letter **M**.

Colour the boxes that show a capital letter **M**.

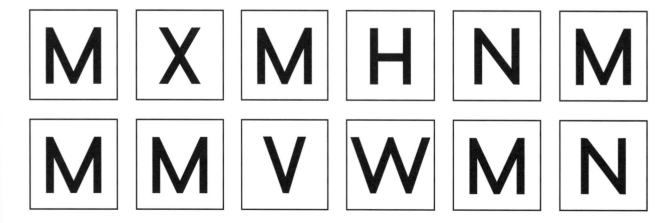

M	X	M	H	N	M
M	M	V	W	M	N

moon

The word **moon** begins
with the lowercase letter **m**.

Colour the circles that show a lowercase letter **m**.

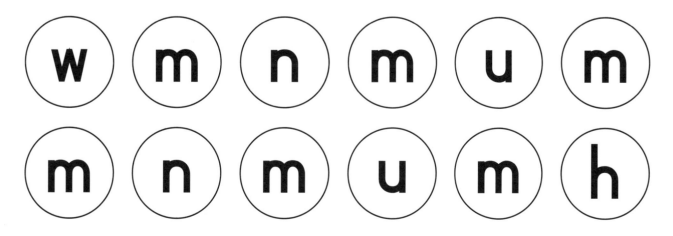

w   m   n   m   u   m

m   n   m   u   m   h

N

Nute Gunray

Nute Gunray begins with the capital letter N.

Colour the boxes that show a capital letter N.

M N H K N W

N H N N Z N

nexu

The word **nexu** begins with the lowercase letter **n**.

Colour the circles that show a lowercase letter **n**.

n a n u m n

n n m b w n

O

Obi-Wan Kenobi

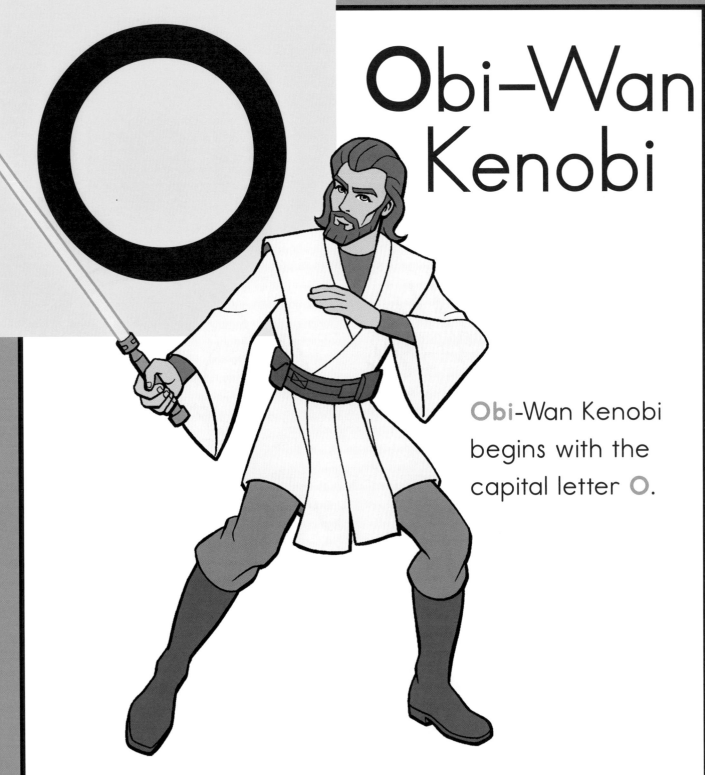

Obi-Wan Kenobi begins with the capital letter O.

Colour the boxes that show a capital letter O.

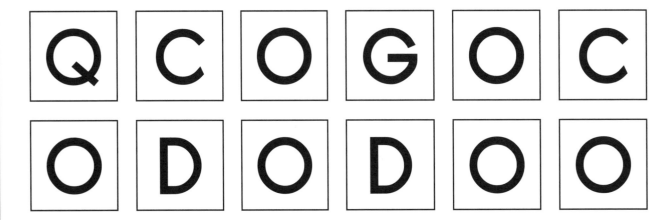

Q C O G O C

O D O D O O

octagon

The word **octagon** begins with the lowercase letter o.

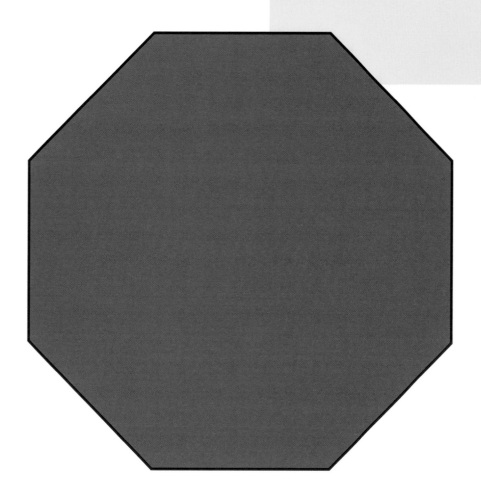

Colour the circles that show a lowercase letter o.

e o c o a o

o o g a o d

P

Princess Leia

Princess Leia begins with the capital letter **P**.

Colour the boxes that show a capital letter **P**.

P	B	H	P	P	B
R	P	P	D	F	P

podracer

The word **podracer** begins with the lowercase letter **p**.

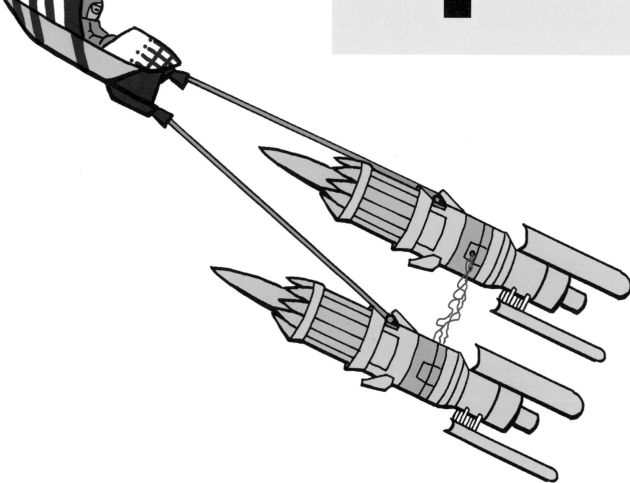

Colour the circles that show a lowercase letter **p**.

p p q g p p

q b d p p q

Q Queen Amidala

Queen Amidala begins with the capital letter Q.

Colour the boxes that show a capital letter Q.

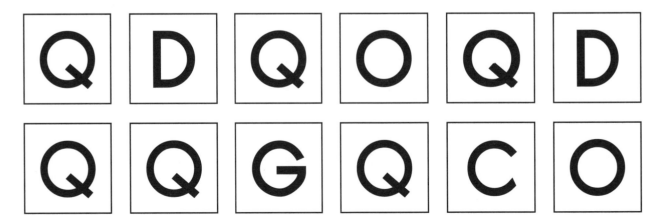

quilt

The word **quilt** begins with the lowercase letter **q**.

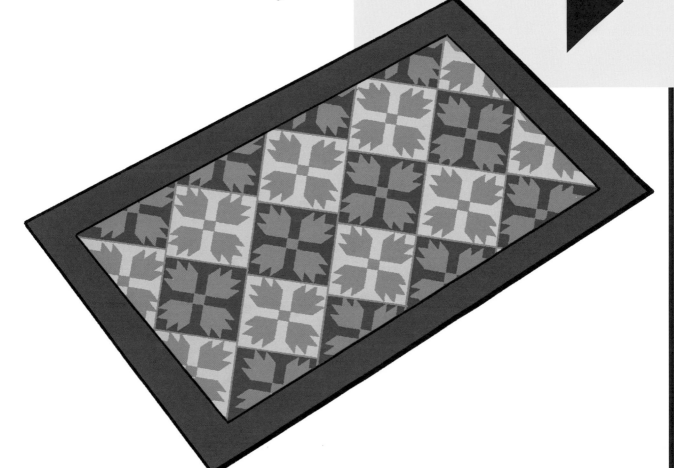

Colour the circles that show a lowercase letter **q**.

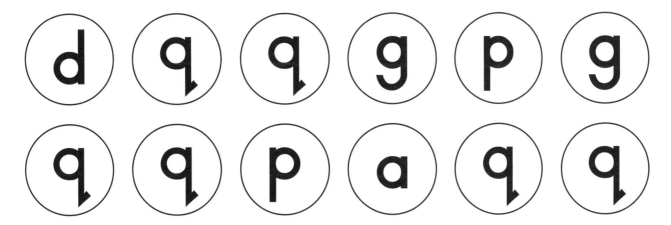

R

Rebel trooper

Rebel trooper begins with the capital letter **R**.

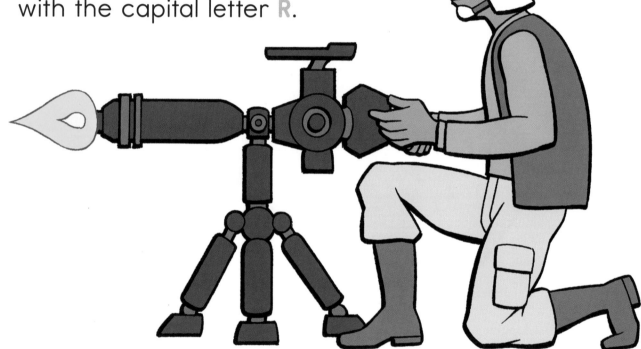

Colour the boxes that show a capital letter **R**.

R	H	R	P	R	R
P	R	B	R	B	D

reek

The word **reek** begins with the lowercase letter **r**.

r

Colour the circles that show a lowercase letter **r**.

r a r c r r

g r n m r c

Let's play match-up!

On the opposite page, say the word for each picture.

What beginning sound do you hear?

Draw a line from each picture to its matching letter.

J

K

L

M

N

O

P

Q

R

S

Storm- trooper

Stormtrooper begins with the capital letter S.

Colour the boxes that show a capital letter S.

S	P	S	S	B	S
F	S	B	S	H	R

star

S

The word **star** begins with the lowercase letter **s**.

Colour the circles that show a lowercase letter **s**.

s   s   a   s   o   z

s   s   c   z   s   c

T

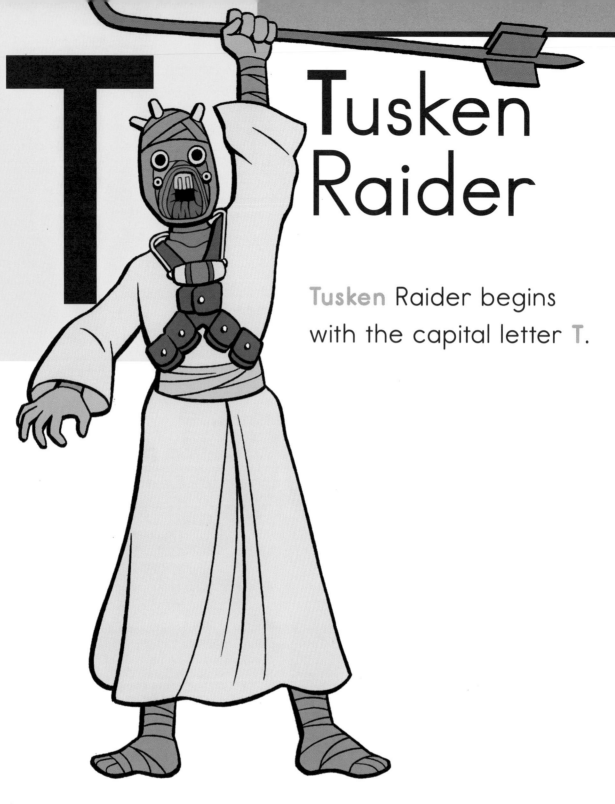

Tusken Raider

Tusken Raider begins with the capital letter T.

Colour the boxes that show a capital letter T.

T	Y	F	T	K	T
H	T	T	L	T	N

tauntaun

The word **tauntaun** begins with the lowercase letter t.

Colour the circles that show a lowercase letter t.

t k t h l t

t a l t f t

U Unduli

Luminara **Unduli**'s last name begins with the capital letter **U**.

Colour the boxes that show a capital letter **U**.

U	V	J	U	U	J
U	H	U	W	U	V

umbrella

The word **umbrella** begins with the lowercase letter **u**.

u

Colour the circles that show a lowercase letter **u**.

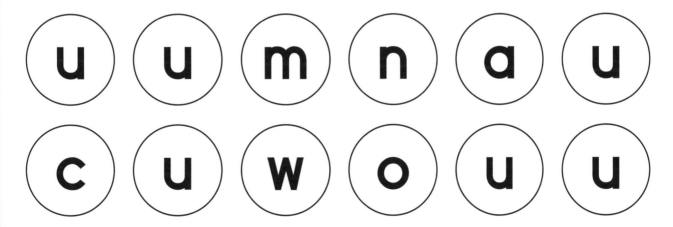

u u m n a u

c u w o u u

V

Vader

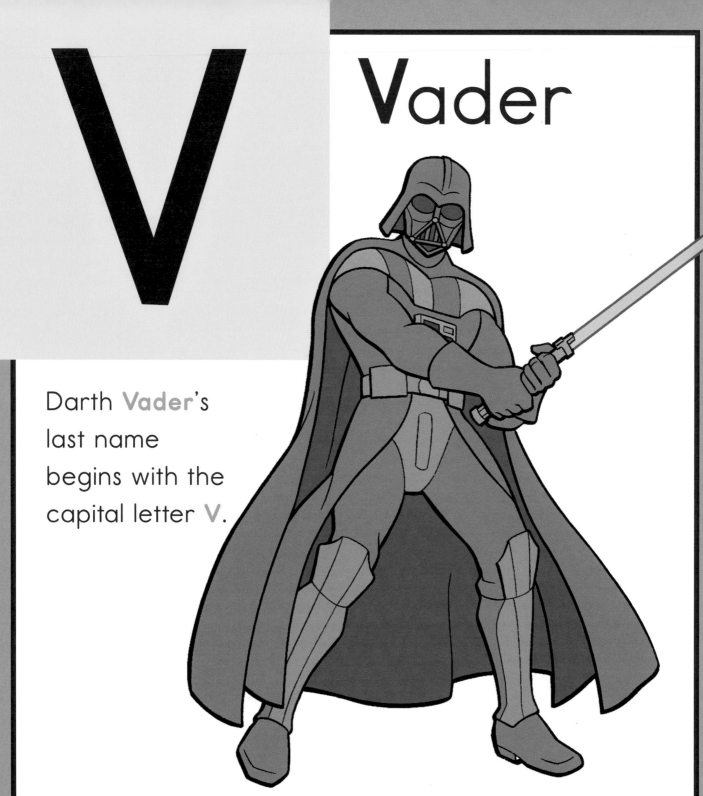

Darth **Vader**'s last name begins with the capital letter V.

Colour the boxes that show a capital letter V.

V	V	X	Y	W	V
N	V	U	V	V	W

volcano

The word **volcano** begins with the lowercase letter **v**.

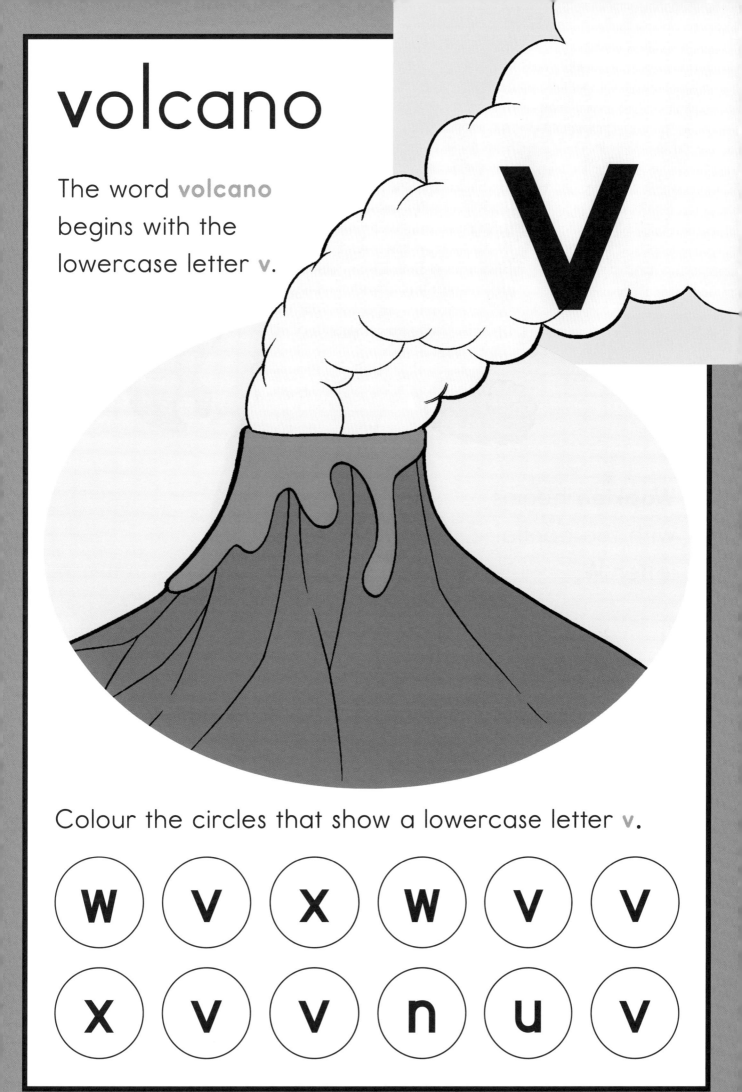

Colour the circles that show a lowercase letter **v**.

W   V   X   W   V   V

X   V   V   n   u   v

W

Wookiee

Wookiee begins with the capital letter **W**.

Colour the boxes that show a capital letter **W**.

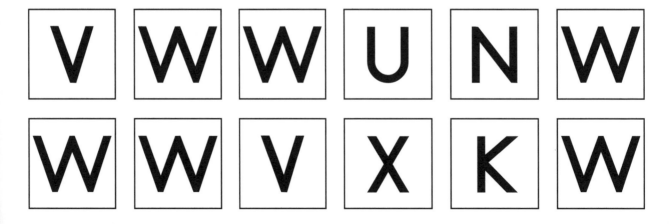

V W W U N W

W W V X K W

wampa

W

The word **wampa** begins with the lowercase letter **w**.

Colour the circles that show a lowercase letter **w**.

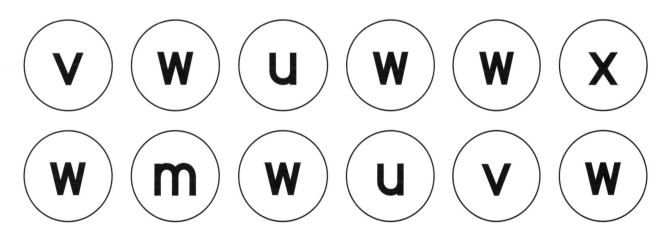

v	w	u	w	w	x
w	m	w	u	v	w

X

X-wing Fighter

X-wing Fighter begins with the capital letter **X**.

Colour the boxes that show a capital letter **X**.

Y	X	K	X	N	X
X	Y	K	X	X	Z

x-ray

The word **x-ray** begins with the lowercase letter **x**.

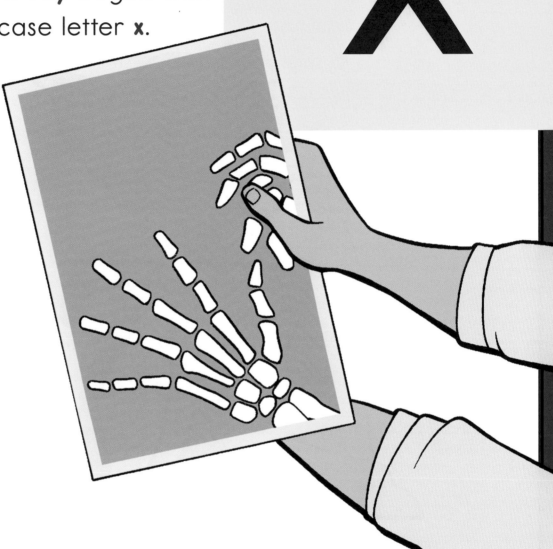

Colour the circles that show a lowercase letter **x**.

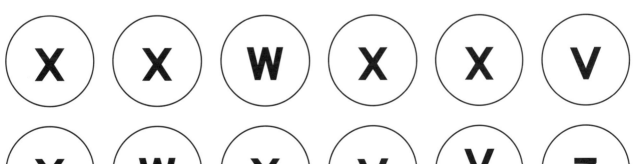

X X W X X V

x W x v y z

Y

Yoda

Yoda begins with the capital letter **Y**.

Colour the boxes that show a capital letter **Y**.

Y	Y	V	H	N	W
V	Y	T	Y	X	Y

youngling

The word **youngling** begins with the lowercase letter **y**.

y

Colour the circles that show a lowercase letter **y**.

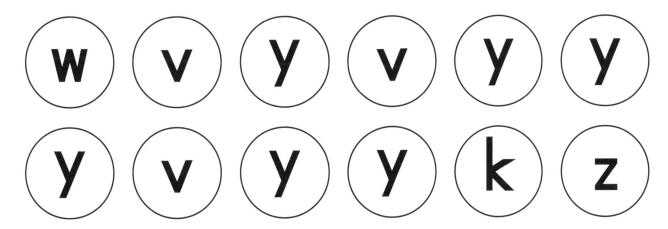

w	v	y	v	y	y
y	v	y	y	k	z

Z

Zam Wesell

Zam Wesell begins with the capital letter **Z**.

Colour the boxes that show a capital letter **Z**.

Z	S	X	Z	H	Z
K	Z	S	Z	Z	Y

zero

The word **zero** begins with the lowercase letter **z**.

Z

0 1 2 3 4
5 6 7 8 9

Colour the circles that show a lowercase letter **z**.

(s) (z) (n) (w) (s) (z)

(z) (z) (a) (z) (z) (n)

Let's play match-up!

On the opposite page, say the word for each picture.

What beginning sound do you hear?

Draw a line from each picture to its matching letter.

S   W

T   X

U   Y

V   Z

You know your ABCs really well!

Now it's time to practise writing your ABCs!

Are you ready?

Let's start with some prewriting!

Prewriting

Trace the dotted lines with your crayon or pencil.

Then draw your own matching lines.

Prewriting

Trace the dotted lines with your crayon or pencil.

Then draw your own matching lines.

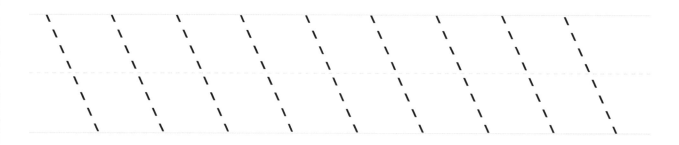

Prewriting

Trace the dotted lines with your crayon or pencil.

Then draw your own matching lines.

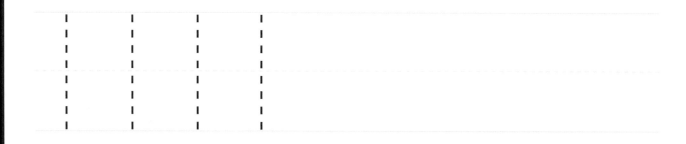

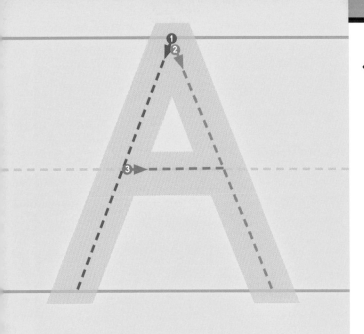

◀ Trace the capital letter A.

Start at the red dot.

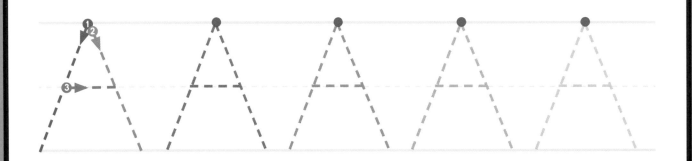

Write the capital letter A inside each box.

Trace the ▶
lowercase letter **a**.

Start at the red dot.

Write the lowercase letter **a** inside each box.

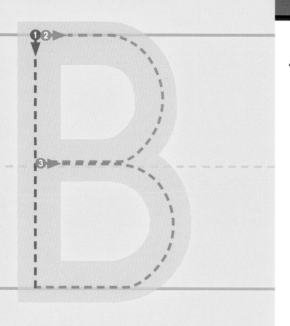

◀ Trace the capital letter **B**.

Start at the red dot.

Write the capital letter **B** inside each box.

Trace the ▶
lowercase letter **b**.

Start at the red dot.

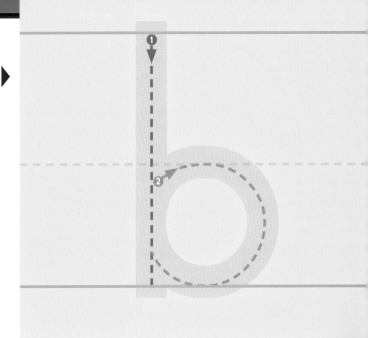

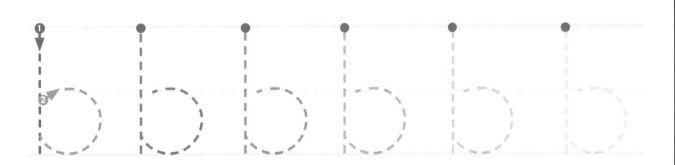

Write the lowercase letter **b** inside each box.

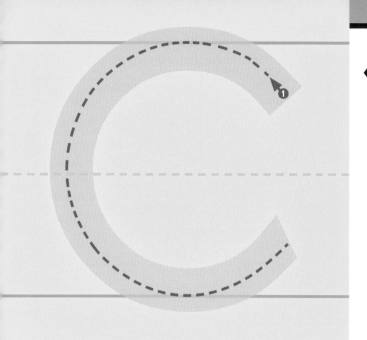

◀ Trace the capital letter C.

Start at the red dot.

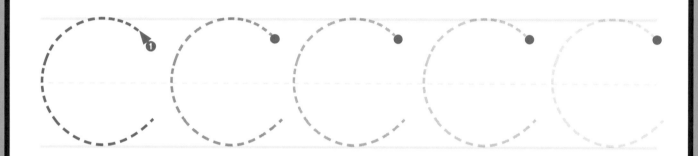

Write the capital letter C inside each box.

Trace the ▶
lowercase letter c.
Start at the red dot.

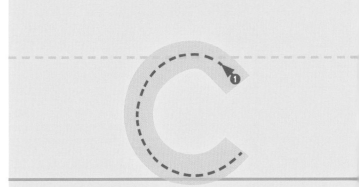

Write the lowercase letter c inside each box.

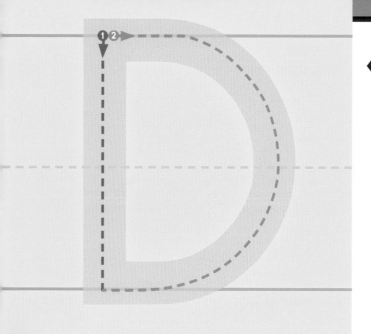

◀ Trace the capital letter **D**.

Start at the red dot.

Write the capital letter **D** inside each box.

Trace the ▶
lowercase letter **d**.

Start at the red dot.

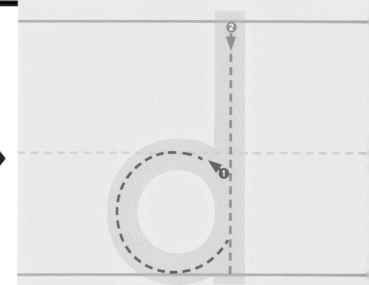

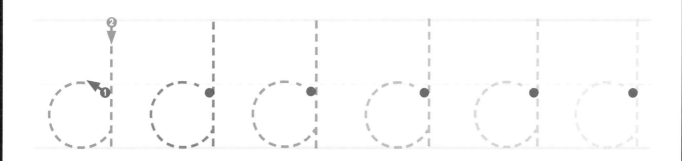

Write the lowercase letter **d** inside each box.

◀ Trace the capital letter E.

Start at the red dot.

Write the capital letter E inside each box.

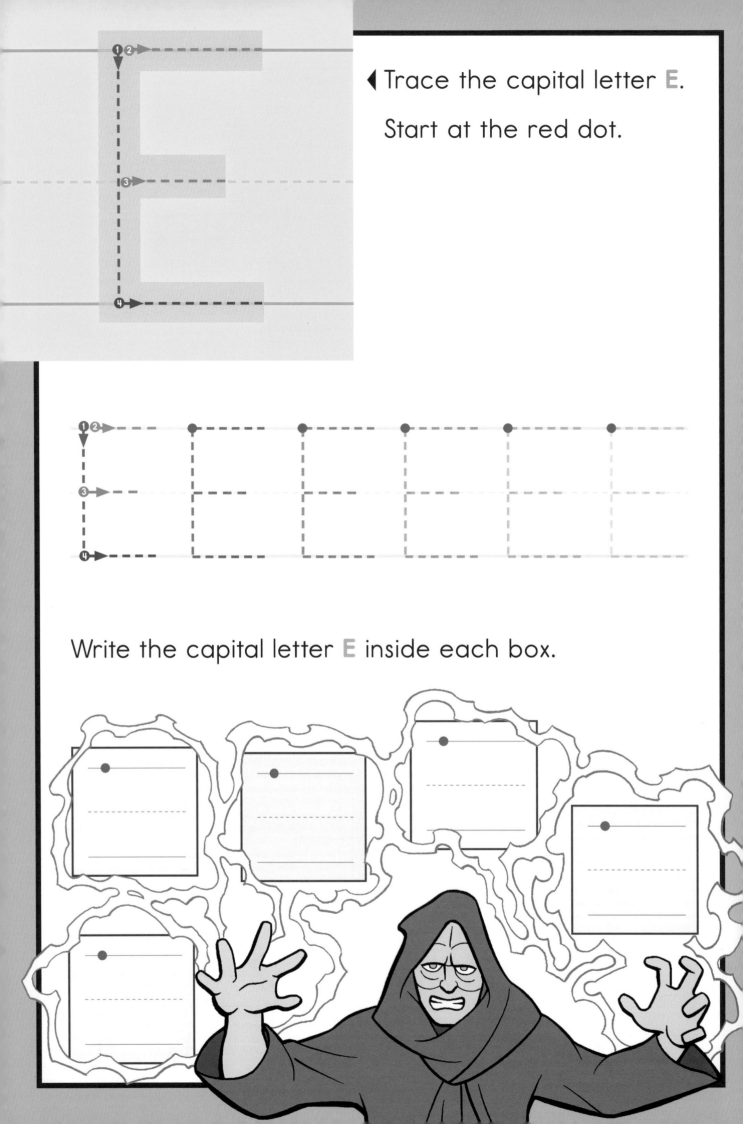

Trace the ▶
lowercase letter e.
Start at the red dot.

Write the lowercase letter e inside each box.

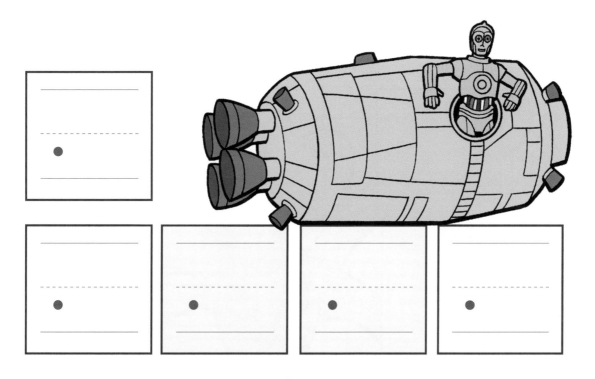

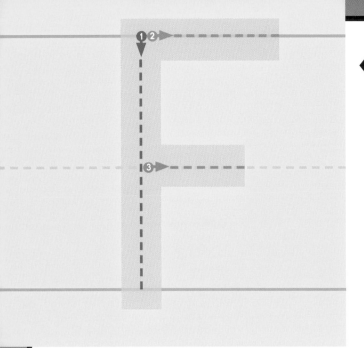

◀ Trace the capital letter **F**.

Start at the red dot.

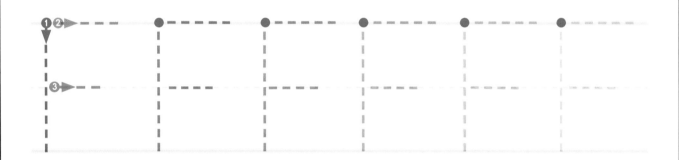

Write the capital letter **F** inside each box.

Trace the ▶
lowercase letter **f**.
Start at the red dot.

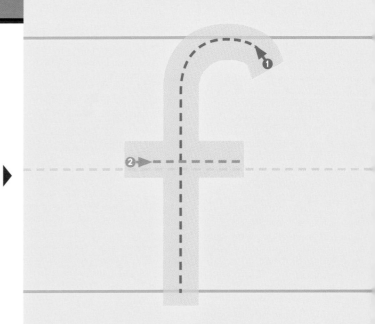

Write the lowercase letter **f** inside each box.

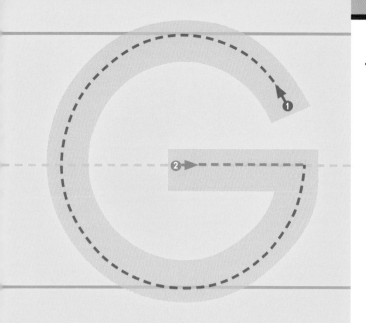

◀ Trace the capital letter G.

Start at the red dot.

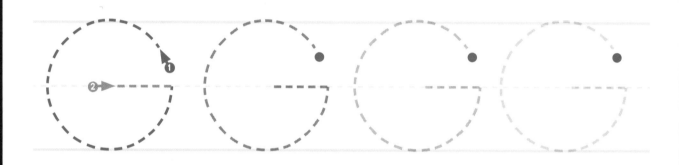

Write the capital letter G inside each box.

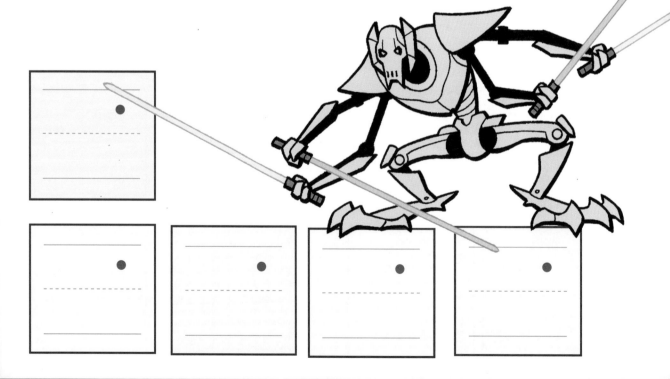

Trace the ▶
lowercase letter **g**.
Start at the red dot.

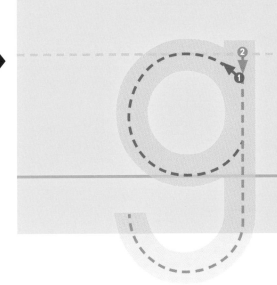

Write the lowercase letter **g** inside each box.

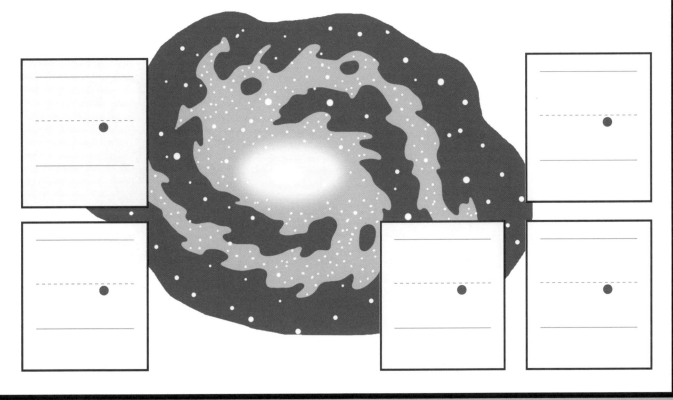

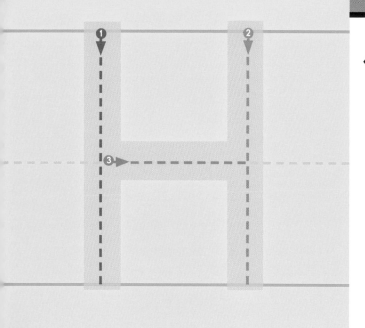

◀ Trace the capital letter **H**.

Start at the red dot.

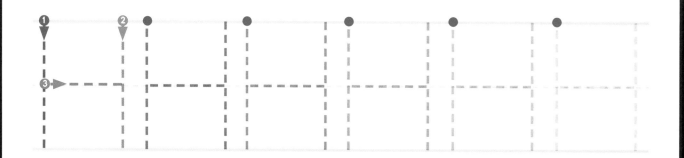

Write the capital letter **H** inside each box.

Trace the ▶
lowercase letter **h**.

Start at the red dot.

Write the lowercase letter **h**
inside each box.

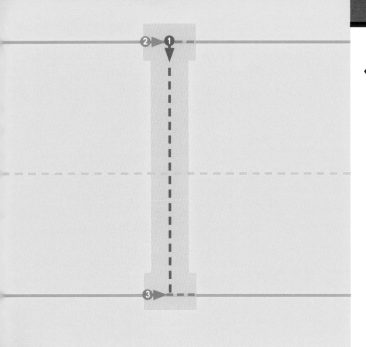

◀ Trace the capital letter **I**.

Start at the red dot.

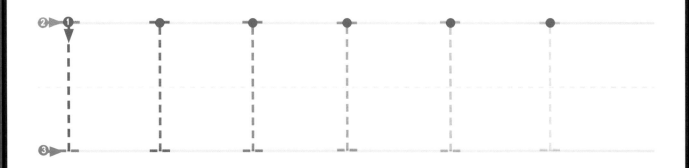

Write the capital letter **I** inside each box.

Trace the ▶
lowercase letter **i**.
Start at the red dot.

Write the lowercase letter **i**
inside each box.

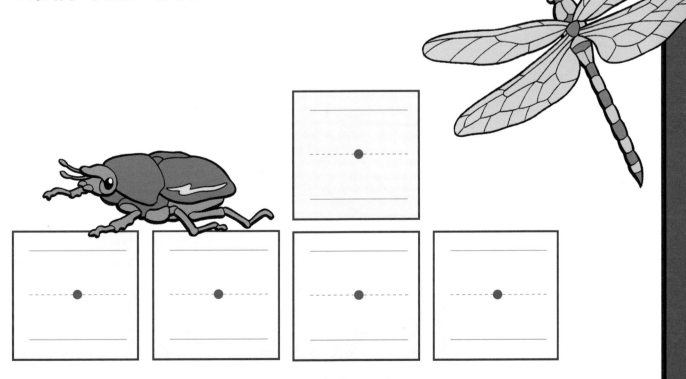

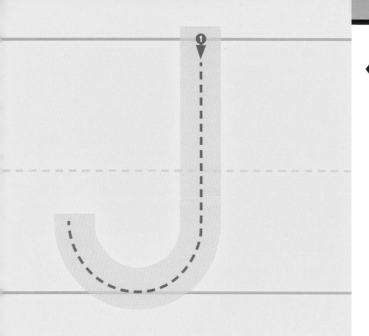

◀ Trace the capital letter J.

Start at the red dot.

Write the capital letter J inside each box.

Trace the ▶
lowercase letter j.
Start at the red dot.

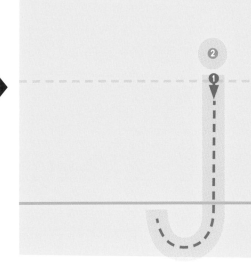

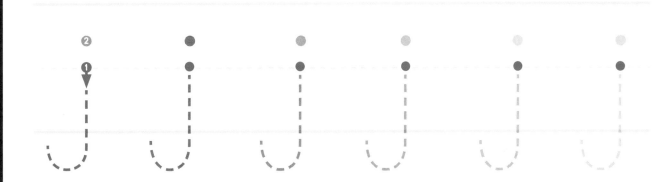

Write the lowercase letter j inside each box.

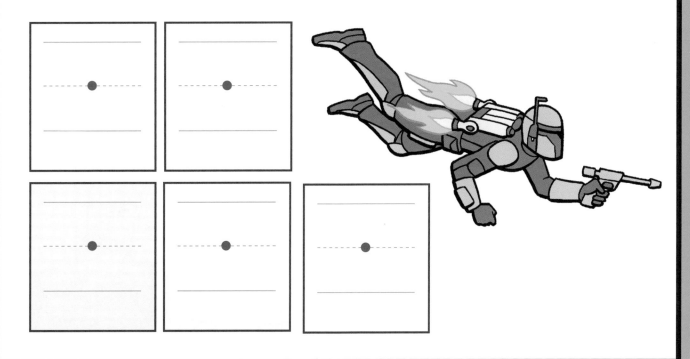

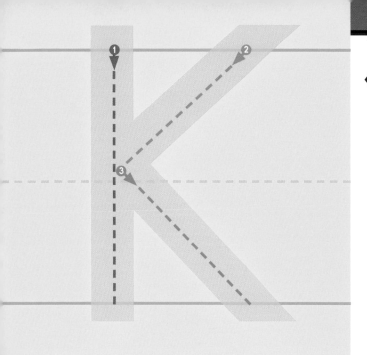

◀ Trace the capital letter **K**.

Start at the red dot.

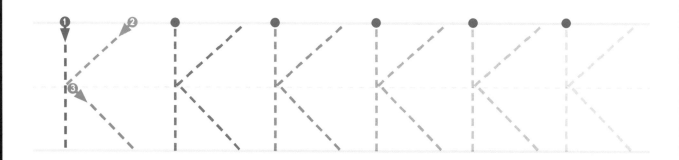

Write the capital letter **K** inside each box.

Trace the ▶
lowercase letter **k**.

Start at the red dot.

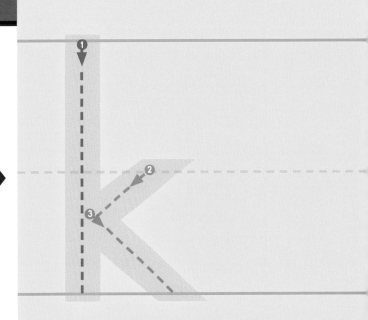

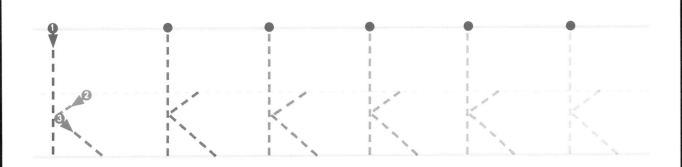

Write the lowercase letter **k** inside each box.

◀ Trace the capital letter L.

Start at the red dot.

Write the capital letter L inside each box.

Trace the ▶
lowercase letter l.
Start at the red dot.

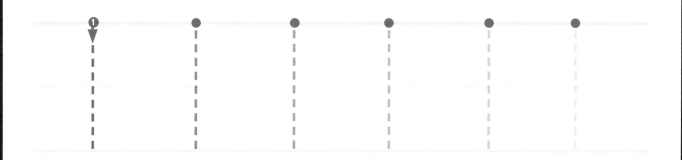

Write the lowercase letter l inside each box.

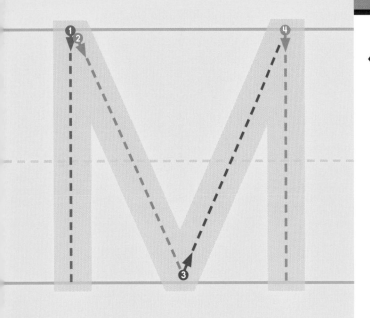

◀ Trace the capital letter **M**.

Start at the red dot.

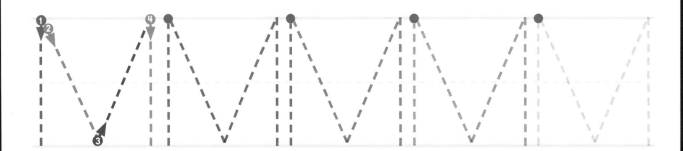

Write the capital letter **M** inside each box.

Trace the ▶
lowercase letter **m**.

Start at the red dot.

Write the lowercase letter **m** inside each box.

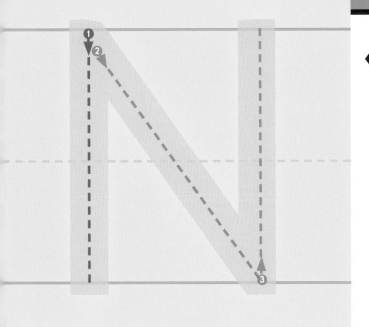

◀ Trace the capital letter **N**.

Start at the red dot.

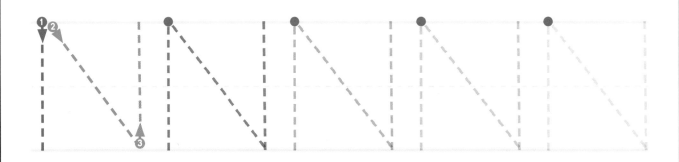

Write the capital letter **N**
inside each box.

Trace the ▶
lowercase letter **n**.
Start at the red dot.

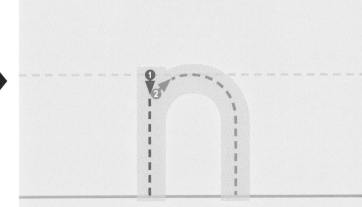

Write the lowercase letter **n**
inside each box.

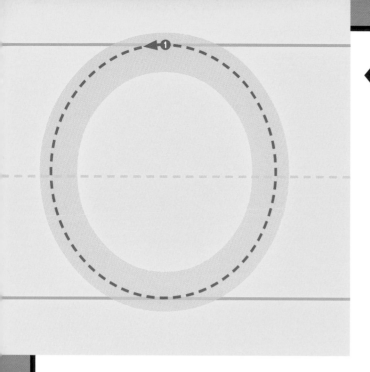

◀ Trace the capital letter O.

Start at the red dot.

Write the capital letter O
inside each box.

Trace the ▶
lowercase letter o.
Start at the red dot.

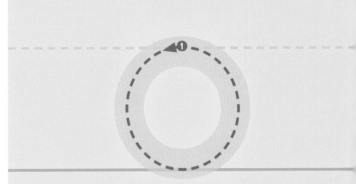

Write the lowercase letter o inside each box.

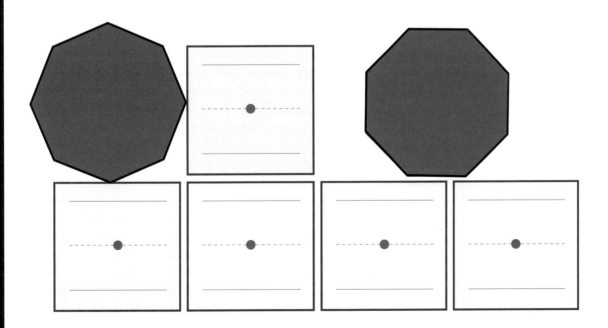

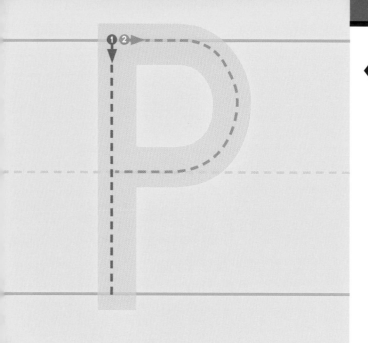

◀ Trace the capital letter **P**.

Start at the red dot.

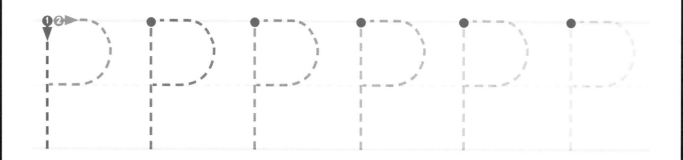

Write the capital letter **P** inside each box.

Trace the ▶
lowercase letter **p**.

Start at the red dot.

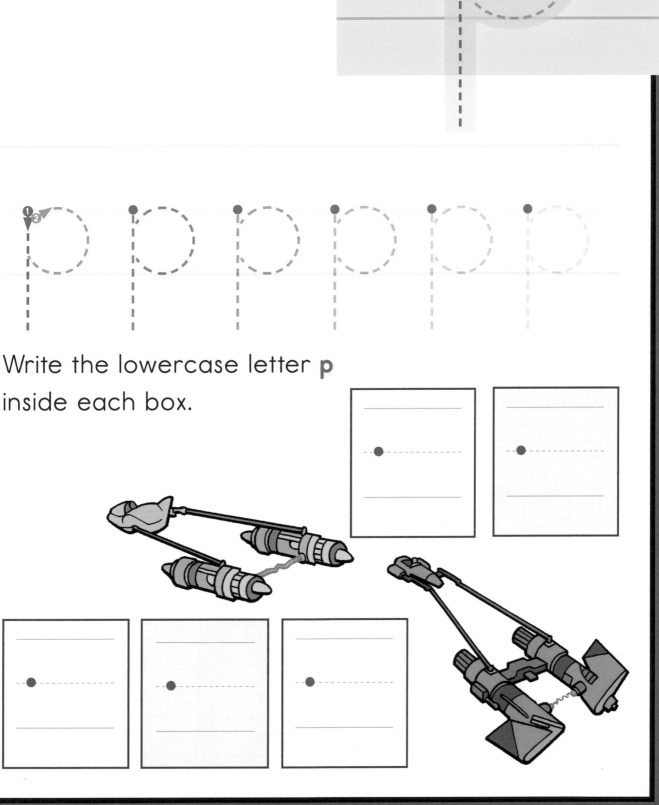

Write the lowercase letter **p**
inside each box.

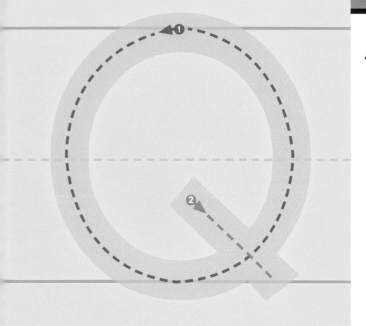

◀ Trace the capital letter **Q**.

Start at the red dot.

Write the capital letter **Q** inside each box.

Trace the ▶
lowercase letter q.
Start at the red dot.

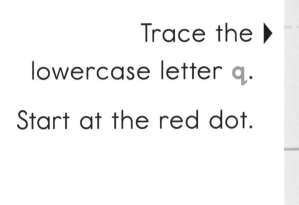

Write the lowercase letter q
inside each box.

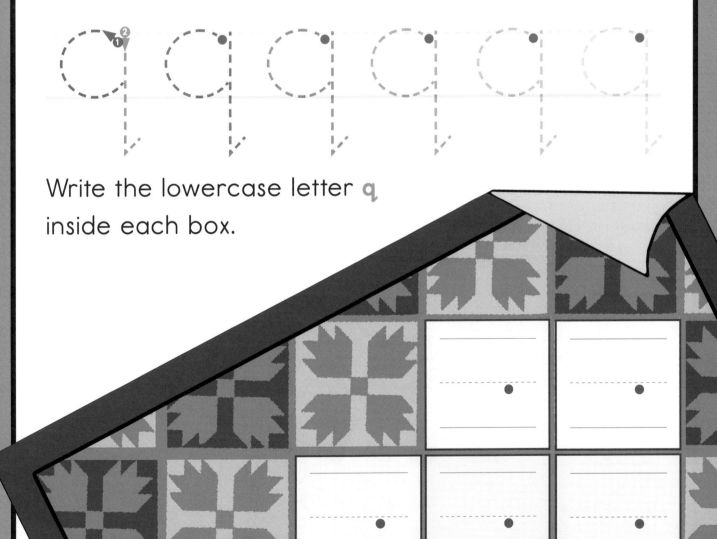

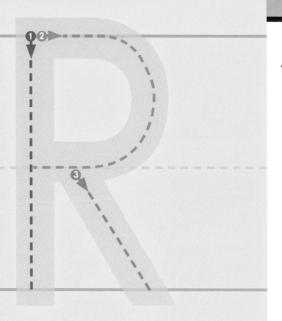

◀ Trace the capital letter **R**.

Start at the red dot.

Write the capital letter **R** inside each box.

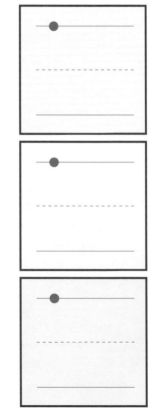

Trace the ▶
lowercase letter r.
Start at the red dot.

Write the lowercase letter r inside each box.

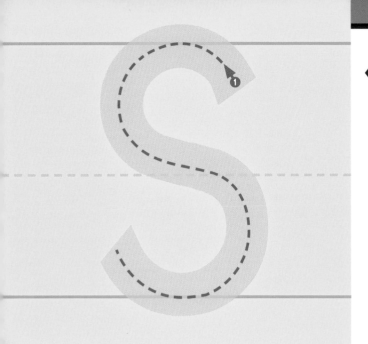

◀ Trace the capital letter **S**.

Start at the red dot.

Write the capital letter **S** inside each box.

Trace the ▶
lowercase letter s.
Start at the red dot.

Write the lowercase
letter s inside each box.

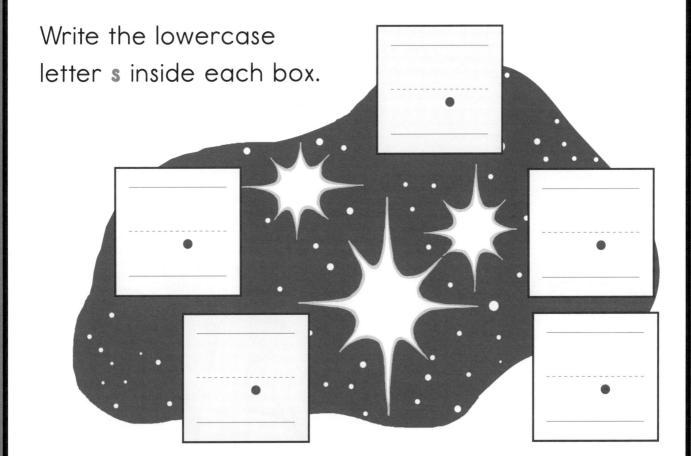

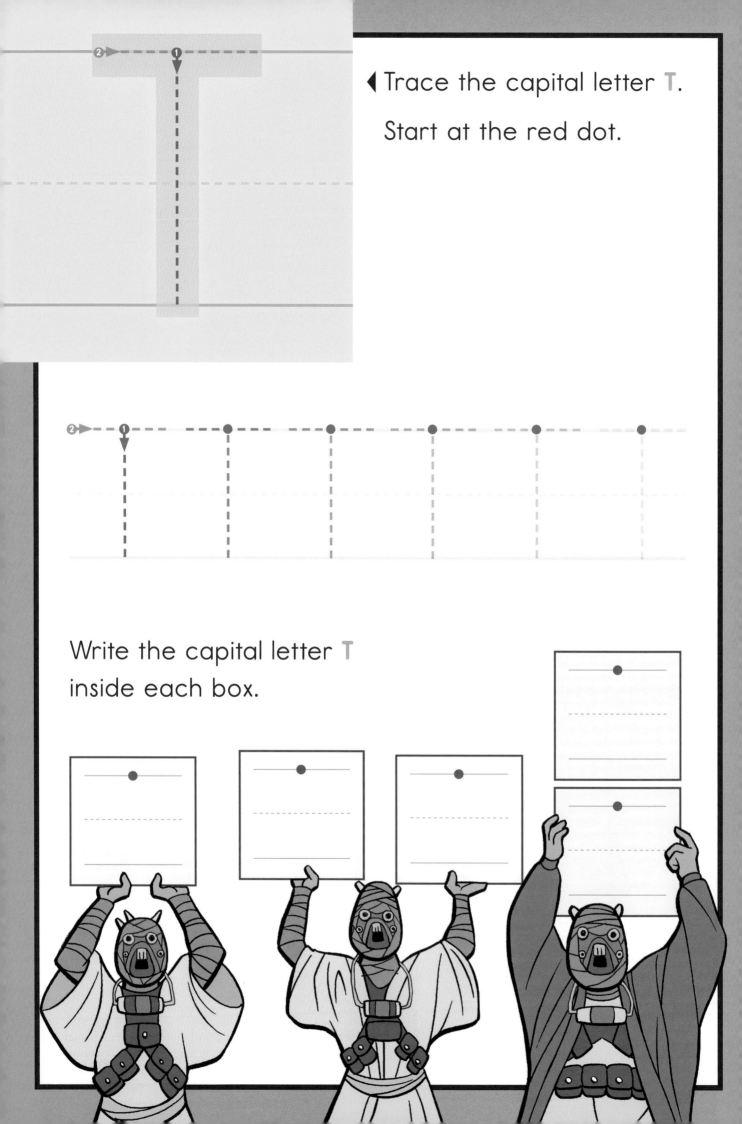

◀ Trace the capital letter T.
Start at the red dot.

Write the capital letter T inside each box.

Trace the ▶
lowercase letter t.
Start at the red dot.

Write the lowercase letter t
inside each box.

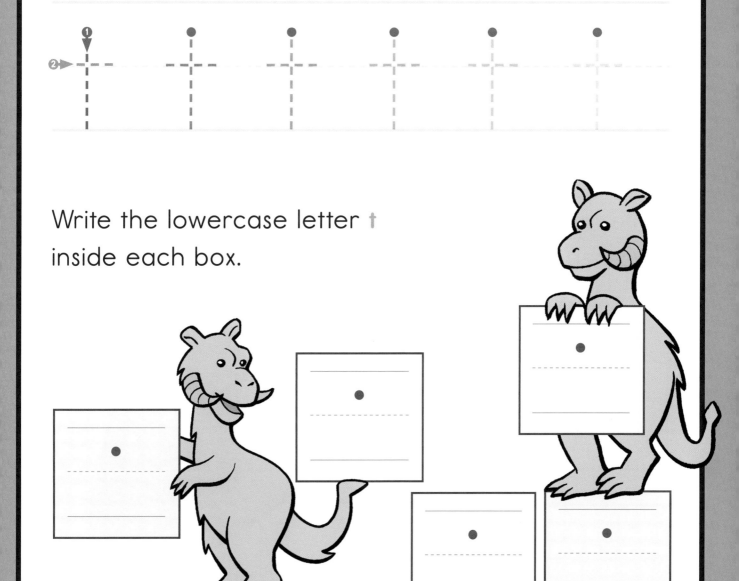

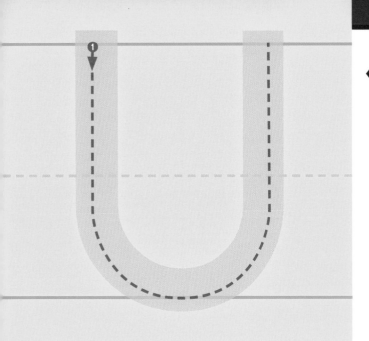

◀ Trace the capital letter **U**.

Start at the red dot.

Write the capital letter **U** inside each box.

Trace the ▶
lowercase letter **u**.
Start at the red dot.

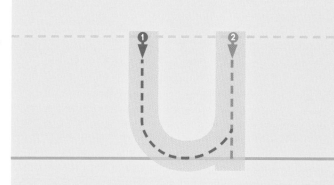

Write the lowercase letter **u** inside each box.

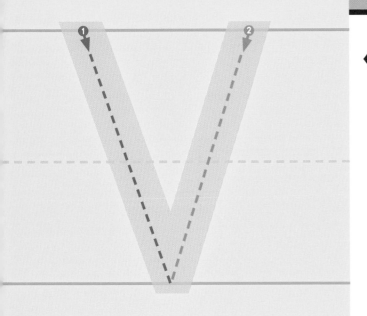

◀ Trace the capital letter V.

Start at the red dot.

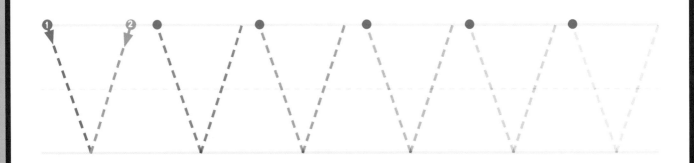

Write the capital letter V inside each box.

Trace the ▶
lowercase letter v.
Start at the red dot.

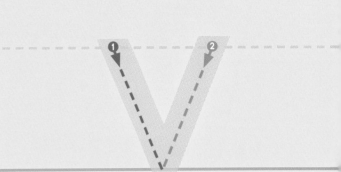

Write the lowercase letter v inside each box.

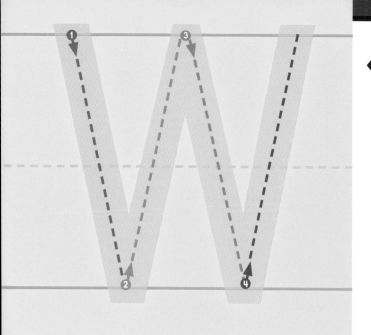

◀ Trace the capital letter **W**.

Start at the red dot.

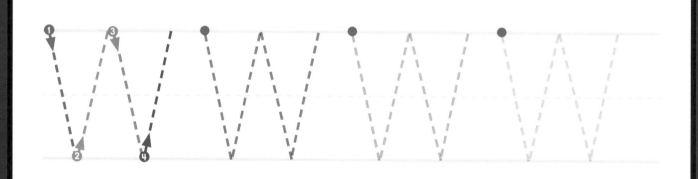

Write the capital letter **W**
inside each box.

Trace the ▶
lowercase letter **w**.

Start at the red dot.

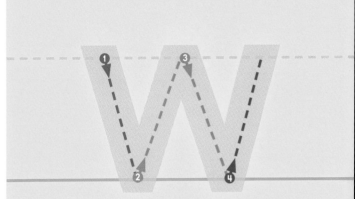

Write the lowercase letter **w**
inside each box.

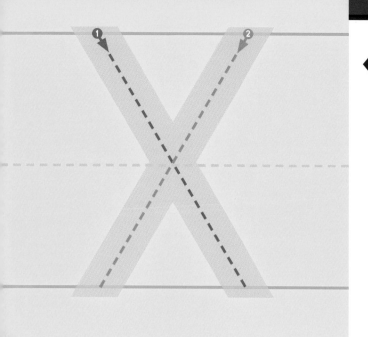

◀ Trace the capital letter **X**.

Start at the red dot.

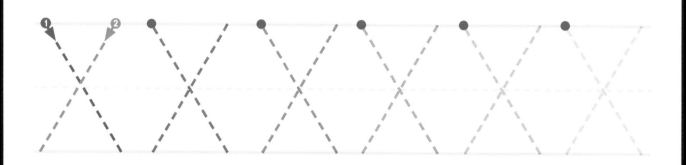

Write the capital letter **X** inside each box.

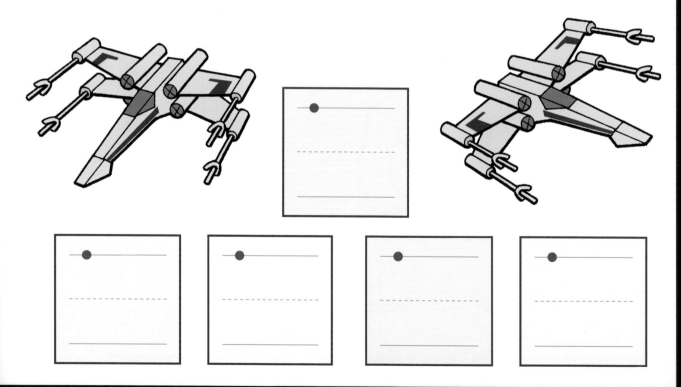

Trace the ▶
lowercase letter **x**.

Start at the red dot.

Write the lowercase letter **x**
inside each box.

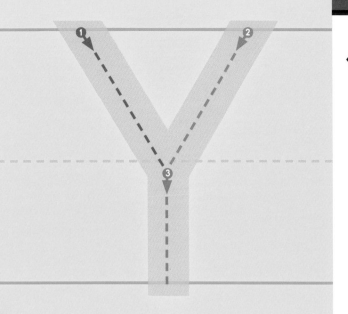

◀ Trace the capital letter **Y**.

Start at the red dot.

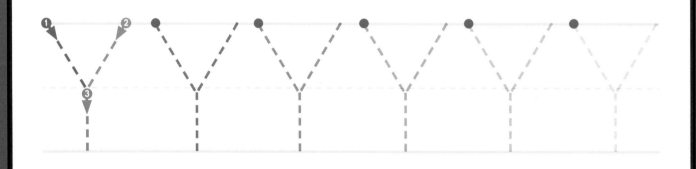

Write the capital letter **Y**
inside each box.

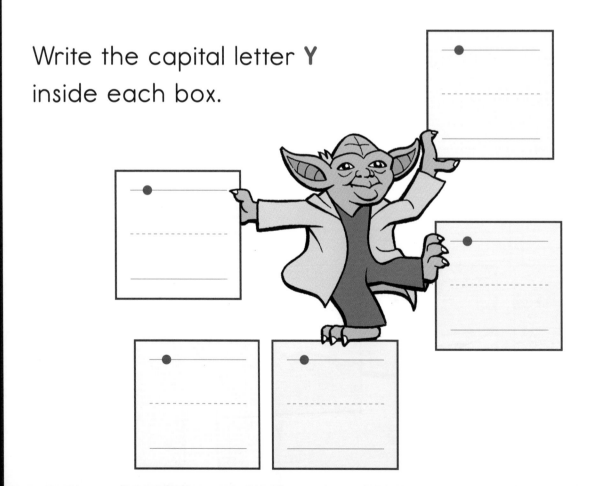

Trace the ▶
lowercase letter y.

Start at the red dot.

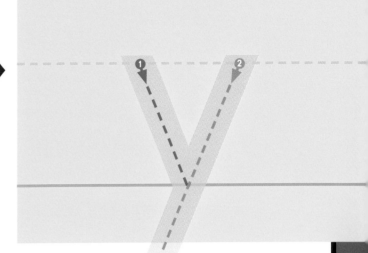

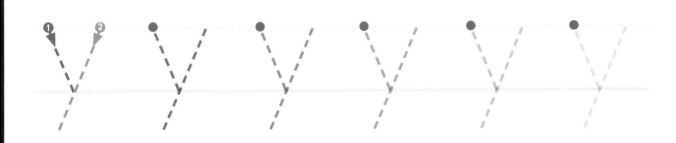

Write the lowercase letter y
inside each box.

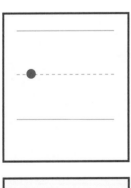

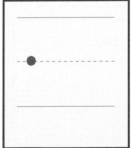

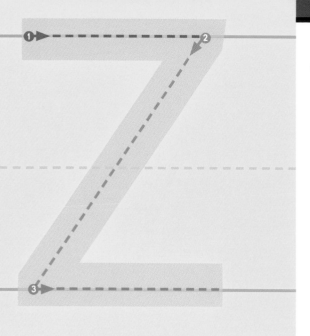

◀ Trace the capital letter **Z**.

Start at the red dot.

Write the capital letter **Z** inside each box.

Trace the ▶
lowercase letter **z**.
Start at the red dot.

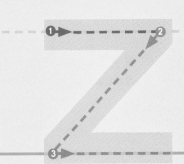

Write the lowercase letter **z**
inside each box.

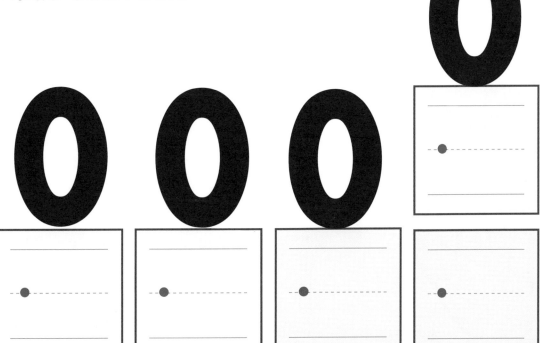

Now you can read and write your ABCs!

Are you ready to have more fun with *Star Wars*?

Make some finger puppets!

Using the templates on the following pages, ask an adult to help you follow the instructions to cut, fold and glue together finger puppet versions of *Star Wars* characters.

What you need:

- Finger puppet templates

- Safety scissors

- Sticky tape or glue

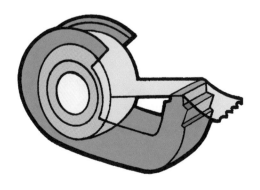

Finger Puppets

1 Ask an adult to cut out each finger puppet.

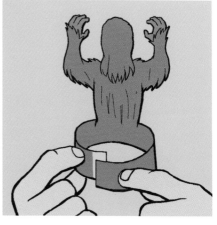

2 Curve the rectangular piece at the bottom of each puppet.

3 Ask an adult to tape or glue together the yellow marked areas.

4 Place finger puppets on your fingers!

TH 23/3/18

Star Wars Workbooks: ABC Fun
Scholastic Ltd
©LFL

Star Wars Workbooks: ABC Fun
Scholastic Ltd
©LFL

Star Wars Workbooks: ABC Fun
Scholastic Ltd
©LFL

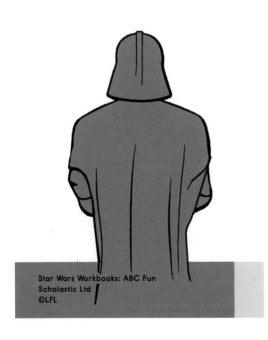

Star Wars Workbooks: ABC Fun
Scholastic Ltd
©LFL

Star Wars Workbooks: ABC Fun
Scholastic Ltd
©LFL